Oxford International English

Student Activity Book

Sarah Snashall

2

OXFORD
UNIVERSITY PRESS

OXFORD
UNIVERSITY PRESS

Great Clarendon Street, Oxford, OX2 6DP, United Kingdom

Oxford University Press is a department of the University of Oxford.

It furthers the University's objective of excellence in research, scholarship, and education by publishing worldwide. Oxford is a registered trade mark of Oxford University Press in the UK and in certain other countries

British Library Cataloguing in Publication Data
Data available

978-0-19-839218-7

21

Paper used in the production of this book is a natural, recyclable product made from wood grown in sustainable forests. The manufacturing process conforms to the environmental regulations of the country of origin.

Printed in India by Multivista Global Pvt. Ltd

Acknowledgements

Cover illustration by Patricia Castelao

Illustrations are by: Roberta Angaramo; Ilias Arahovits; Micha Archer; Beatrice Bencivenni; George Black; Patricia Castelao; Katriona Chapman; Pippa Curnick; Steve Dorado; Steve Horrocks; Cathy Ionescu; Alan Marks; Meg Hunt; Jonatronix; Tamara Joubert; Mike Love; Gustavo Mazali; Jess Mikhail; Zack Mcloughlin; Dusan Pavlic; Luciana Navarro Powell; Kristina Swarner.

The publishers would like to thank the following for permissions to use their photographs:

p6: Photodisc; p10-11: Photodisc; p16: Pavel K/Shutterstock; p16: Tibor Bognar/Alamy; p16: PhotoBliss/Alamy; p18: svry/Shutterstock; p21: Deyan Georgiev/Shutterstock; P34: Blue Jean Images / Alamy; p34: Bubbles Photolibrary/Alamy; p34: John Birdsall/AGE Fotostock; p43: mtkan/Shutterstock; p48: Glow Asia RF/Alamy; p48: auremar/Shutterstock; p48: alexkar08/Shutterstock; p53: Photodisc; p56: cobalt88/Shutterstock; p57: Jon Stuart; p66: sad444/Shutterstock; p66: Peter Stroh / Alamy; p66: aclav Volrab/Shutterstock; p70: iadams/Shutterstock; p76: Ken Lucas/Getty; p76: Franco Banfi/naturepl.com; p76: Sergey Uryadnikov /Shutterstock; p77: Jason Isley-Scubazoo/Science Faction/Corbis; p78: Eduard Kyslynskyy/iStockphoto.com; p80: Juniors Bildarchiv GmbH/Alamy; p84: David Keith Jones/ALAMY; p86: Julie Langford/www.limbewildlife.org;

Although we have made every effort to trace and contact all copyright holders before publication this has not been possible in all cases. If notified, the publisher will rectify any errors or omissions at the earliest opportunity.

Links to third party websites are provided by Oxford in good faith and for information only. Oxford disclaims any responsibility for the materials contained in any third party website referenced in this work.

Welcome to Activity Book 2. We'll help you along the way.

Contents

Unit contents

Unit	Theme	Reading and comprehension	Writing
1	New friends	**Fiction** Narrative with a familiar setting *The Dreaming Tree*	Fiction Planning a story with setting, characters and structure story with beginning, middle and end
2	Party time!	**Non-fiction** Instructions *Party To Do list, Invitation, How to get to my house, How to Make a Pizza, The Great Coin Trick, Dancing Dragon Puppet, Catch the Dragon's Tail game*	Non-fiction Writing instructions
3	Everyday poems	**Poems** Playtime poems *On the Playground, My Football Counting Rhyme, My Mum's Sari, Goodbye Granny, Supermarket*	Poetry Writing a poem
4	World stories	**Fiction** Traditional narratives from around the world *How Bear Lost His Tail, The Golden Slipper, Yoshi the Stonecutter*	Fiction Writing a traditional story
5	How things work	**Non-fiction** Explanations *How Glass is Recycled, Exploring Volcanoes, How to Create a 3D World*	Non-fiction Writing an explanation
6	Caribbean trip	**Poems** Poems by significant poets *I'd Like to Squeeze, Flying Fish, Classes Under the Trees, Water Everywhere, Crab Dance, Granny Granny Please Comb My Hair*	Poetry Writing a poem
7	Mountain bear adventure	**Fiction** Narrative by significant author *The Dancing Bear*	Fiction Planning a story with a sequence of events Evaluate and edit story plan
8	Animal world	**Non-fiction** Non-chronological reports *Amazing Leatherback Turtle Facts, Animals in Danger, Young Explorers, Ngorongoro Crater*	Non-fiction Writing report facts
9	Wordplay poems	**Poems** Poems with language play *Over My Toes, Allivator, Tree Poem, Name That Dragon, Night-lights, Sheep*	Poetry Writing a list poem

Language, grammar, spelling, vocabulary, phonics, punctuation	Speaking and listening
• Blend sounds • Connectives, *and, but, because* • Two-letter phoneme, /ar/ • Extending range of interesting words and phrases to describe	Questions – developing ideas and explaining further Recounting experiences Expressing ideas precisely
• Instructions vocabulary • Common suffix, –*ly* • Blend sounds • New words in context	Questions – developing ideas and explaining further Expressing ideas precisely Including relevant details Attentive listening and role play
• Rhyming patterns • Long vowel phonemes /igh/ /ee/ /oa/ /ai/ /oi/ /oo/ • New words in context • Alliteration • Features of poetry genre	Questions – developing ideas and explaining further Expressing ideas precisely Trying out different ways of speaking Speak clearly about likes and dislikes in reading poetry
• Long vowel phoneme, /ou/ • Connectives, *but, when, because, and* • Verbs past tense • Traditional tale language • Compound words • Interesting words and phrases to describe people • Significant words • Respond to question words	Questions – developing ideas and extending understanding Recounting experiences Expressing ideas precisely Including relevant details Vary talk to hold listener's attention Show attentive listening
• Long vowel phonemes, /ee/ /ai/ /igh/ • Time words • Sentence punctuation: capital letters • Verbs • Connectives, *so, because* • Interesting and significant words and phrases • Features of explanation texts • Question words	Questions – developing ideas and extending understanding Recounting experiences Expressing ideas precisely Including relevant details
• Rhyming words, sounds and rhythm • Alliteration • Spelling common word ending, –*ing* • Interesting and significant words and phrases • Features of poetry genre • Adjectives • Compound words	Expressing ideas precisely Including relevant details Listening carefully, responding and asking questions of others
• Common suffix, –*ly* • Simple adverbs • Language of time • Time words • Interesting and significant words and phrases • New words in context	Questions – developing ideas and extending understanding Expressing opinions and ideas precisely
• Features of non-chronological reports • Finding factual information from charts and diagrams • Verbs • Significant and technical words • Subheadings and paragraphs • Syllables • Connectives, *and, if, because, when* • Adjectives	Questions – developing ideas and extending understanding Expressing opinions and ideas precisely
• Digraph, *sl* • Rhyming words • Features of poetry genre • Adjectives • Common spellings of /igh/ phoneme	Extending experiences through role-play Reciting poems Expressing opinions precisely

1 New friends

Let's Talk

What does it feel like to move to a new place?

The Dreaming Tree

 **A** **Read and respond**

Write the things Roberto links in his mind to Rio de Janeiro and the ones he links to Ireland. Find the words in the story.

> **trees and flowers**   **warm and sunny weather**
>
> **grandmother**   **parrots**   **park**   **snakes**   **rain**

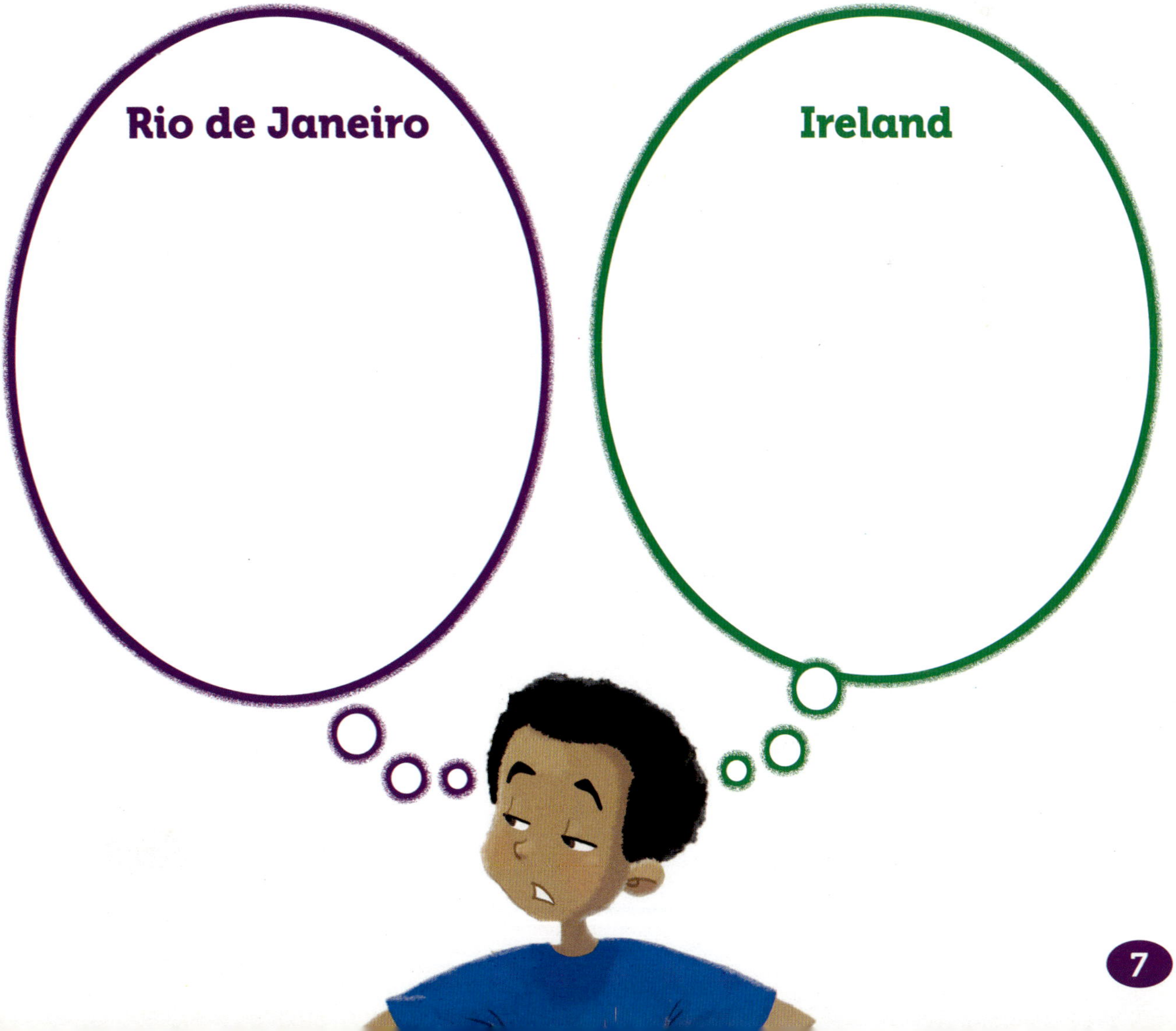

Rio de Janeiro

Ireland

B Read and respond

Find clues in the story to show how Roberto feels at the beginning and the end of the story and write them in the boxes.

Beginning

End

C What do you think?

Answer these questions.

1 Why was Roberto walking quickly at the beginning of the story?

_____

2 How do you think Roberto felt when he watched the boys playing football?

_____

3 Why did Vovó tell Roberto the story of the Dreaming Tree?

_____

_____

4 What is Roberto's heart's desire?

_____

5 Roberto showed off his Brazil top at the end of the story. What does this tell the reader about how he is feeling?

_____

_____

Word detective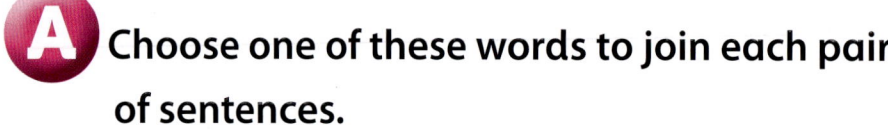

A Choose one of these words to join each pair of sentences.

> **and   but   because**

1 *Amanda smiled most of the time. She was not smiling now.*

Amanda smiled most of the time _____ she was not smiling now.

2 *He wanted to get through the park quickly. He did not want to see the boys playing football.*

He wanted to get through the park quickly _____ he did not want to see the boys playing football.

3 *He was always the captain. He always got the best players.*

He was always the captain _____ he always got the best players.

4 *Roberto and Amanda always spoke Portuguese to their grandmother. She didn't speak any English at all.*

Roberto and Amanda always spoke Portuguese to their grandmother _____ she didn't speak any English at all.

B Find words in the story that have the letter group **ar** in them. Put them in the correct column.

If you find more words for any column, write them on a separate piece of paper.

ar at the beginning of the word, e.g. **ar**t	**ar** in the middle of the word, e.g. p**ar**t	**ar** at the end of the word, e.g. f**ar**

C Find three words or phrases in the story that describe the park and three that describe the jaguar. Then add two of your own for each one.

The park   **The jaguar**

_____   _____

_____   _____

_____   _____

Your own words

_____   _____

_____   _____

Get writing

Plan a story set somewhere you know well.

Part A Familiar setting

Choose one of these settings for your story.

Describe your chosen setting here.

_____

_____

_____

_____

_____

Don't forget to use adjectives to describe your setting.

Part B Main character

Draw your character

What is your character like? (Shy, kind, funny, silly, naughty, mean, sensible or something else?)

_____

What does your character like to do? (Play sports, read, chat on the phone, draw, play computer games or something else?)

_____

What is your character's name?

_____

What is their heart's desire?

_____

Part C Story plan

Use these questions to help you to plan your story. Write your plan on separate paper.

Beginning

Where is your character? What is he or she doing? Do they see something?

Middle

What happens next? Does your character get lost? Do they meet someone? Do they get given something? Do they feel frightened or excited?

End

How does your story finish?

Use your plan to tell your story to your partner.

2 Party time!

How to get to my house

A Read and respond

1   Use the street map on page 21 in the anthology. Start at the school and follow these directions.

Turn left out of the school. Take the first turning on the left. Carry on to the next corner. Cross over the road. Where are you?

_____

2   Your mother wants to buy some bread on the way to the party. Write directions for getting from the school to the bakery.

_____

_____

_____

3   Choose a place on the map. Give your partner directions to get there from the school. Make sure you use these time words: First, Next, Then.

Did your partner end up at the right place?

Word detective

A Find four instruction words in How to Make a Pizza.
Write them here.

_____   _____

_____   _____

Find these three time words in How to Make a Pizza.
Tick them when you had found them.

First ☐   Next ☐   Finally ☐

Words ending in **–ly** often tell us how something is done.

B Find one word in The Great Coin Trick that ends in **–ly**.

_____

C Place a tick in the chart when you find each feature in the instructions you have read.

	Party To Do list	How to get to my house	How to Make a Pizza	The Great Coin Trick
Instruction words				
Numbered points				
What you need list				
Clear language				
Diagrams				

Clear language makes instructions easy to understand.

 **A** Read and respond

Answer these questions about Dancing Dragon Puppet.

1 Why do you need a pair of scissors?

_____

2 When do you need to use sticky tape?

_____

3 What do you use the straws for?

_____

 **B** Read and respond

Use the picture to help you write the instructions.

_____ _____ the

_____ _____ and

_____ .

C Read and respond

Number the instructions in the correct order for the Catch the Dragon's Tail game. Instruction 1 has been done for you.

1 Divide yourselves into two teams.

Each dragon head chases the other dragon's tail.

The first dragon to pull out the other dragon's tail is the winner.

Hold on to the shoulders of the child in front of you.

The two dragon tails tuck their scarves into their waist bands.

Word detective

A Write four instruction words from Dancing Dragon Puppet.

_____

_____

B Find these words in Dancing Dragon Puppet. With a partner, talk about what you think they mean.

direction   **concertina**   **secure**

C Write an instruction word for each of these actions.

_____stir_____   _____

_____

_____

_____

_____

_____

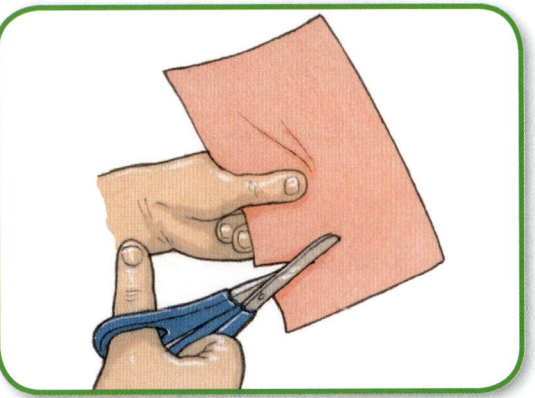

_____

Get writing

My pizza

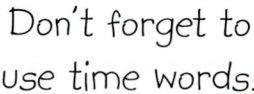

Don't forget to use time words.

 **A** Write instructions for making a pizza.

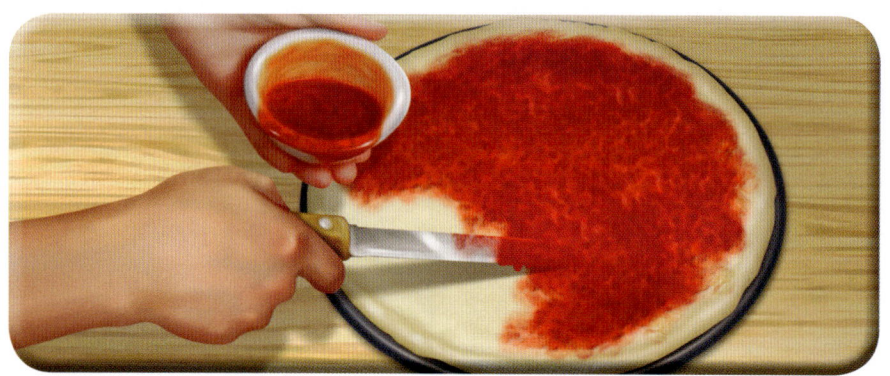

How to make a Chinese lantern

B Write the instructions next to each picture.

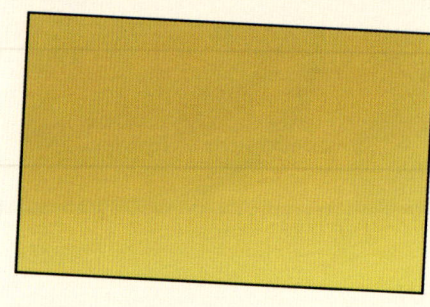
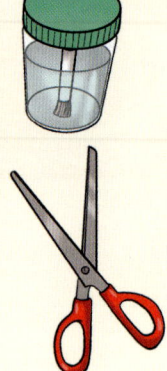

You will need

Coloured paper

Scissors

Glue

- Cut some lines along the fold end.
- Fold the paper in half.
- Stick the handle on the inside of the lantern.
- Cut a strip of paper to make a handle. Put glue on each end.
- Open out the paper. Glue the short sides together.

What to do

1 _____

_____

_____

2 _____

_____

_____

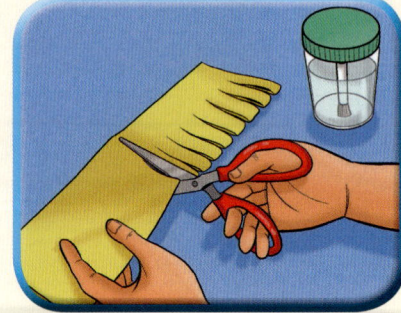

3 _____

_____

_____

4 _____

_____

_____

_____

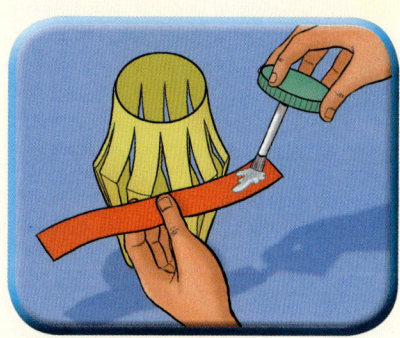

5 _____

_____

_____

Make more lanterns and hang them up!

27

Everyday poems

A Read and respond

Read **On the Playground** and **My Football Counting Rhyme**. With a partner, say which poem you like best and why.

B Read and respond

Reread **My Football Counting Rhyme**. Tick the box to show if each sentence is true or false.

	True	False
He kicked the football six times in the kitchen.	☐	☐
The football smashed the greenhouse glass.	☐	☐
He had to hide the football.	☐	☐

C What do you think?

In **My Football Counting Rhyme**, the boy says he had to hide. Do you think this was right, or should he have owned up to breaking the glass?

_____

_____

Word detective

A Find words in My Football Counting Rhyme that rhyme. With your partner, talk about the rhyming pattern.

B Long vowel sounds can be spelled out by different letter groups. Say these sounds to practise. With a partner, take turns to think of a word for each long vowel sound and spell it out.

/igh/   /ee/   /oa/

/ai/   /oi/   /oo/

C Draw a line between each pair of rhyming words. Underline the different ways the long vowel sound is spelt in each pair. The first one has been done for you.

w<u>ee</u>p	toys
wait	bite
sight	l<u>ea</u>p
coat	wrote
boot	plate
noise	fruit

My Mum's Sari

A **Read and respond**

Write down one thing that the child loves to do with her mum's sari.

_____

B **Read and respond**

What does 'quick escape' mean in the last line of the poem?

_____

C **Read and respond**

In the poem, find two words together that start with the same sound.

_____   _____

When two words that start with the same letter and sound are placed together, it makes the poem sound interesting.

Goodbye Granny

 A Read and respond

Does the boy live close to Granny? How do you know?

_____

_____

B Read and respond

Where do you think the good times are stored?

_____

_____

C Read and respond

Find words that start with the same sound that sit next to each other in the poem.

_____   _____

Supermarket

 ## Read and respond

With a partner, take on the roles of Joe and his mother. Each time his mother repeats his name, make your voice louder.

 ## Read and respond

With your partner, work out what happens to the jam, the cans and the Chocolate Dreams at the end of the poem.

 ## Read and respond

Find the following types of poems in this unit and write their names. (You can use the same poem more than once.)

Can you find…?	Name of poem
A poem that rhymes	_____
A poem with a strong rhythm	_____
A poem that paints pictures in your mind	_____
A funny poem	_____

Get writing

A Using the three-line pattern that is used in **On the Playground** write a two verse poem about being back in the classroom after playtime.

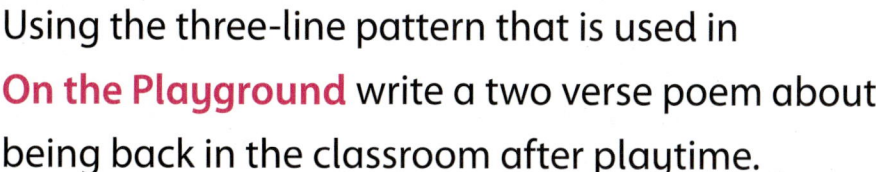

You can use some of these rhyming words to help you.

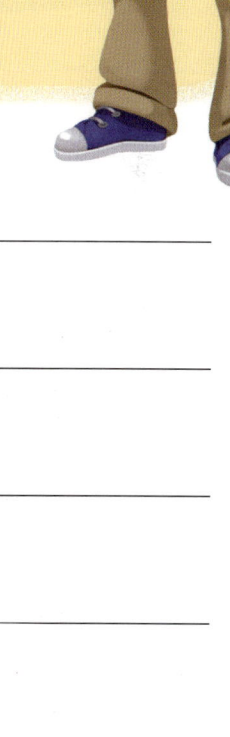

snoring	drawing	storing
talking	walking	squawking
playing	saying	laying
throwing	sowing	blowing

_____

_____

_____

_____

_____

_____

 **World stories**

Let's Talk

What is your favourite story? Is there someone in your family who tells you stories?

How Bear Lost His Tail

 **Read and respond**

Use the story map to tell your version of the story to a friend.

1

2

3 Fox grabbed the fish and ran off with it.

4 Fox lied to Bear about how he caught the fish.

5 Bear put his tail in the icy water.

6

7 Bear was angry and went off to find Fox.

B Read and respond

Draw a line from each character to the word that best describes their personality.

Fox

Bear

kind

trusting

trickster

silly

C What do you think?

Why do you think Fox was so mean to Bear?

_____

_____

Word detective

A Circle all the words that have the **/ou/** sound in them.

> plough   snow   how   frozen
>
> mountain   cold   cough   now
>
> count   growl   nowhere

B Fill in the missing connective in each sentence.

> but   when   because   and

1   Fox was tired and hungry _____ he saw the fish that Otter had caught.

2   Bear sat down _____ put his tail in the water.

3   Bear's tail tingled _____ the water was so cold.

4   Bear looked at his tail _____ it had come off!

 **Find the right verbs from the story to complete these sentences.**

Snow _____ everything. There _____

frost on the berries and ice _____ the lake and

Fox and Bear _____ _____ anything

to eat.

Otter _____ to see his friend and _____

his fish down. But Fox _____ the fish in his

sharp teeth and _____ off with it.

Add a past tense verb of your own in each sentence.

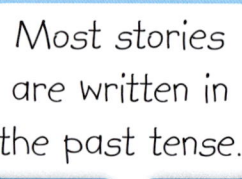

Most stories are written in the past tense.

Otter _____ surprised.

The animals _____ for food.

Bear _____ with anger.

The Golden Slipper

 **Read and respond**

Find four phrases that tell you this story is set in a different time and place from your own.

_____

_____

_____

_____

B **Read and respond**

With a partner, pretend to be Hutun and her daughter after Maha gets married. What do they say to each other?

Do you think they are happy for Maha?

39

C Read and respond

Answer these questions.

1 Why was the stepmother mean to Maha?

_____

2 Why was the red fish kind to Maha?

_____

3 What did the fish mean when it said that Maha's beauty was her kind heart?

_____

_____

 **A** Find these words in the story. Split each word into the two words that make it.

fisherman _____ _____

friendship _____ _____

throughout _____ _____

everyone _____ _____

sunrise _____ _____

Words like these are called compound words.

B Point out all the time words and phrases in the story to your partner.

Yoshi the Stonecutter

 **Read and respond**

Yoshi finds out what really makes him happy. What does he *think* will make him happy? Complete these sentences.

1 When Yoshi is a stonecutter he wants to be a rich man

because _____

2 When Yoshi is a rich man he wants to be a prince because

_____

3 When Yoshi is a prince he wants to be the sun because

_____

4 When Yoshi is the sun he wants to be a cloud because

_____

5 When Yoshi is a cloud he wants to be a rock because

_____

6 When Yoshi is a rock he wants to be a stonecutter because

_____

B Read and respond

What kind of person is Yoshi? Think of your own words to describe him.

_____

_____

_____

_____

_____

_____

C What do you think?

What would you wish for that would make you happy?

_____

_____

Do people, places, events or objects make you happy?

43

Word detective

Find at least four of each of these types of words in the three stories you have read.

Words that show time passing

Words for 'said'

Words for movement

Get writing

Write the next part to the story How Bear Lost His Tail in which kind Otter teaches Bear to fish for salmon by a waterfall.

Part A

Look at this snowy scene. Imagine you are there. Use the words to help you write a description of the scene. How would you write this to start your story?

paw prints in the snow

frozen lake

thick snow

branches laden with snow

_____

_____

_____

_____

Part B

What kind of personalities do Otter and Bear have?
Write some words to describe them in the boxes.

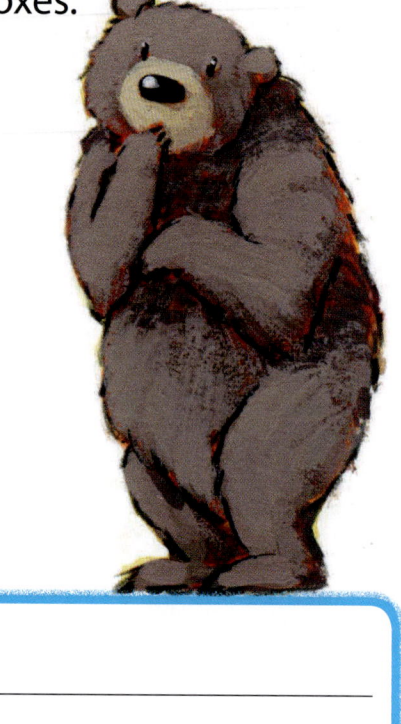

Part C

Plan your story. Write the words and phrases you are going to use under each picture. Use a separate piece of paper if you want to write more.

Title of story: _____

How things work

Let's Talk

What was the last explanation you gave?

How Glass is Recycled

There are two types of explanation text:
- Explaining **how** things work or happen
- Explaining **why** things work or happen

 **A** Read and respond

Which type of explanation text is this?

_____

B Read and respond

Answer these questions.

1 How is glass sorted when it first reaches the recycling plant?

_____

2 What is the third thing that happens to glass bottles and jars when they are being recycled?

_____

3 What happens to the glass after it has been melted?

_____

C Read and respond

Think about the order in which glass is recycled.

1 Write these words in the correct order
to show how glass is recycled.

sorted   shaped   cleaned   melted

_____

2 How does the author show the order of the steps in the
recycling process?

_____

_____

Word detective

 **A** Find a word in the text that has the long:

/ee/ sound _____

/ai/ sound _____

/igh/ sound _____

B Add one of these time words to each sentence.

finally   then   first

Don't forget to change the first letter to a capital letter when the word starts the sentence.

1 _____ the glass bottles are collected.

2 The bottles are _____ sorted into different colours.

3 The glass is washed, melted and _____ made into new glass.

C Underline the verbs in these sentences.

1 Jars are put into the bin.

2 Bottles are put together.

3 The glass is melted.

Remember – these verbs are made up of two parts.

Exploring Volcanoes

A **Read and respond**

Answer these questions.

1 What is a volcano?

_____

_____

2 Why do scientists use a robot to explore inside a volcano?

_____

3 What happens in the control room?

_____

_____

4 Name one thing that makes Dante II good for exploring volcanoes.

_____

_____

B Read and respond

Does this text explain how something works or happens, why something works or happens, or both?

C Read and respond

Draw a line from the information to the section you find it in.

Information	Section
General information about volcanoes	Chart (page 51)
Dangerous volcanoes around the world	A close-up of Dante II diagram (page 53)
The parts of Dante II	Introduction (page 50)
Information about the people who live near Mount Vesuvius	Caption to photo (page 50)

Word detective

A **connective** is a word that joins two parts of a sentence together.

A Choose the best connective to complete each sentence.

so   because

1 Dante II has eight legs _____ it can climb over rocky ground.

2 Dante II can walk over rocky ground _____ it has eight legs.

3 Dante II has a video camera _____ it can take pictures.

4 People use a robot to explore inside volcanoes

_____ it is not safe for them to go inside.

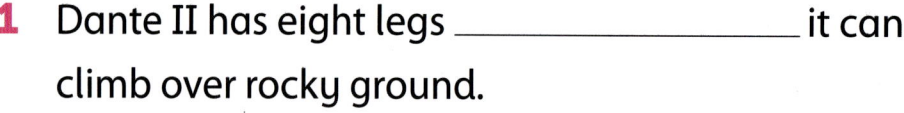

How to Create a 3D World

**A** **Read and respond**

Number these actions to show the order in which Jon does them.

◯ Jon moves the eyes of the character.

◯ He puts the character into a pose.

◯ Jon creates the character's expression.

◯ He puts skin and clothes on the skeleton.

◯ He puts the character into a setting.

◯ Jon creates the skeleton for the character.

B **Read and respond**

Find two phrases that make the explanation sound interesting for the reader.

_____

_____

Word detective

A Tick each of these features of explanation texts when you find it in **How to Create a 3D World**.

Present tense ☐   Illustration ☐

Time words ☐   Technical words ☐

> Why do you think explanations have pictures?

B Explanations often use technical words. Find these technical words. Talk to a partner about what they mean.

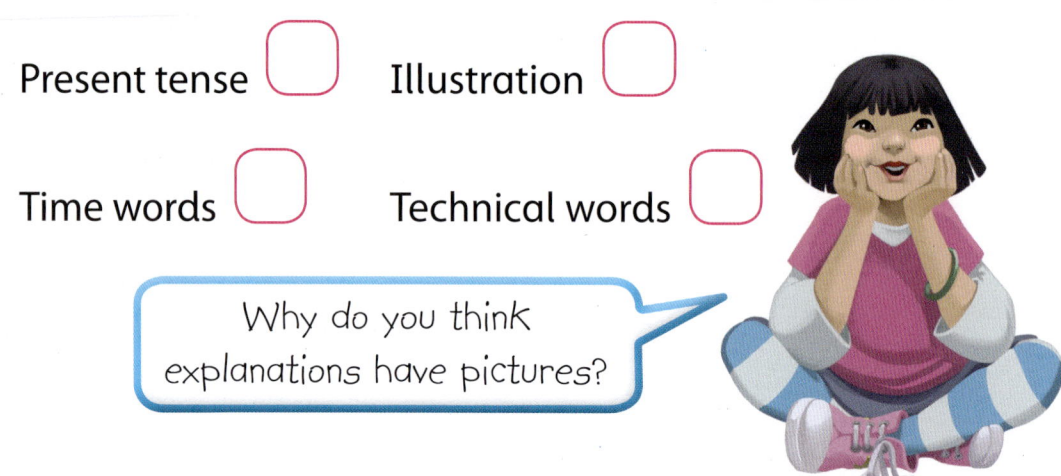

illustrations

pose

skeleton

gadgets

C Imagine you are going to interview Jon Stuart about his work.

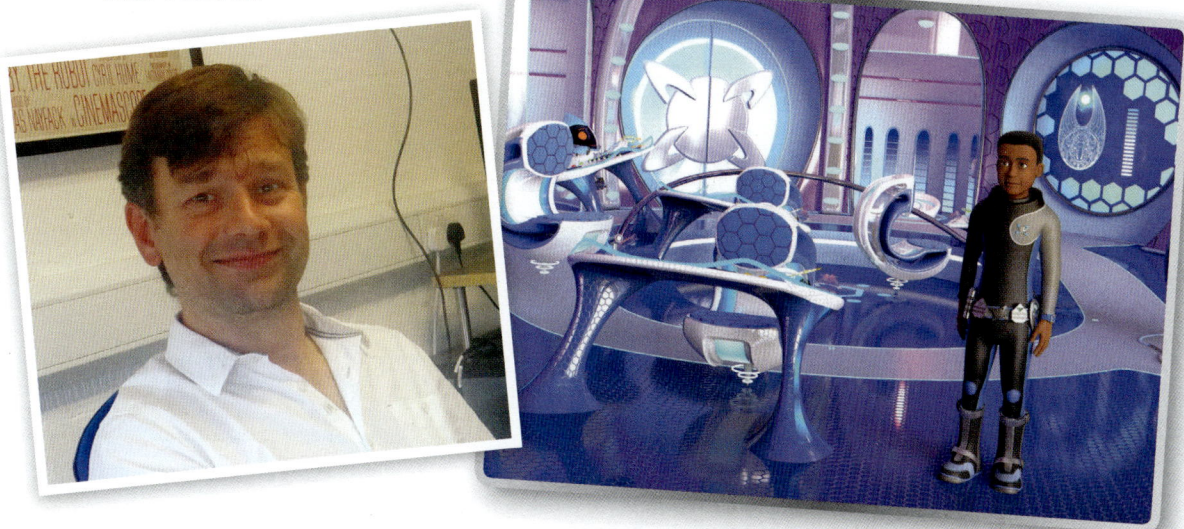

What questions would you like to ask him?

What _____

When _____

How _____

Where _____

Who _____

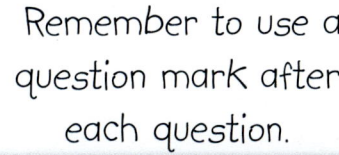

Remember to use a question mark after each question.

57

Get writing

How a toast-making machine works

Part 1

Use these words to label this diagram of a toast-making machine.

chopper   toaster   butter   plate   conveyer belt

Part 2

How does the machine work? Write your explanation here.

First, the bread is toasted and pops out _____

_____

Next, _____

_____

Then, _____

_____

Finally, _____

_____

Flying Fish

 A Read and respond

Answer these questions.

1 How does the fish move in the water?

_____

2 How does the fish move in the air?

_____

3 Do you think the flying fish needs to make up its mind?

_____

B Read and respond

Describe the scene to your partner.

C What do you think?

Choose your favourite line. Explain why you like it.

_____

Word detective

A Find one pair of rhyming words.

_____   _____

B Find one line that uses alliteration.

_____

C Add **–ing** to these words. Cross out any letters that need to be removed.

If the word ends in 'e', remove the 'e' before adding **–ing**.

fly _____   dance _____

slither _____   creep _____

race _____   peck _____

Classes Under the Trees

 Read and respond

Answer these questions.

1 Why does the class go outside?

_____

2 When do they have their lessons outside?

_____

3 Why does the poet think that the birds are having their lessons?

_____

_____

B Read and respond

Find words or a phrase that help to create a picture in your head.

_____

C Read and respond

This poem doesn't rhyme. Discuss with your partner what makes it a poem.

Word detective

A Find two interesting adjectives in the poem.

> Remember – an **adjective** describes a person, a place or a thing.

_____

_____

B Find three compound words. Write the two words that make up each one. Discuss with your partner how they help you understand the meaning of the word.

1 _____   _____ =

_____

2 _____   _____ =

_____

3 _____   _____ =

_____

Crab Dance

A Read and respond

Answer these questions.

1 When do the red crabs come out to dance?

_____

2 Where do the red crabs go to dance?

_____

3 What patterns can you see in each verse?

_____

_____

B Read and respond

Talk to your partner about why 'scuttle-foot', 'side-ways' and 'bulb-eye' are good ways to describe the way the crabs move.

C What do you think?

Discuss with your partner why the poet chose this setting and time to describe the crabs' dance.

Get writing

A Write a poem about fish swimming in the moonlight.
Use these words – or your own – to complete the verse.

silvery

sparkling

glistening

darting

Play moonlight

and the _____ _____ dance

their _____ dance

in the _____ sea.

**Write a second verse about children dancing
on the beach.**

Play sunlight

and the _____ _____ dance

their _____ dance

on the _____ sand.

7 Mountain bear adventure

Let's Talk

Do you think wild animals should be kept as pets?

The Dancing Bear

 **Read and respond**

Answer these questions.

1 Where is the story set?

_____

2 Who is telling the story?

_____

3 How does Roxanne's grandfather make money from the bear?

_____

_____

4 If Roxanne goes with Niki to become a pop star, what do you think will happen to Bruno?

_____

_____

67

B Read and respond

1 Write what you think the characters might be thinking.

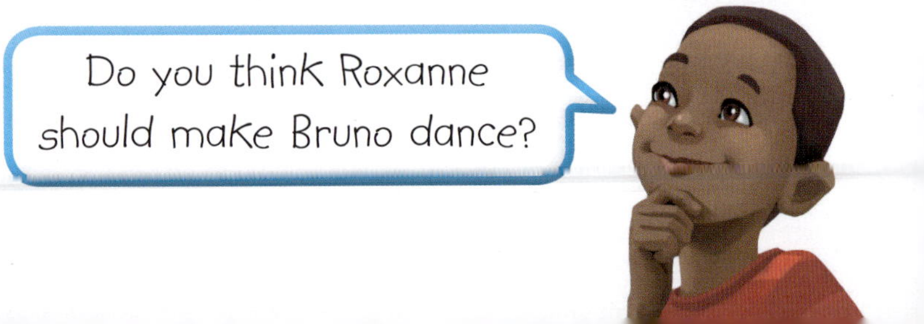

Do you think Roxanne should make Bruno dance?

2 **Circle the three statements that are true.**

a Grandfather lets Roxanne keep the bear because he wants Roxanne to have a pet.

b The bear makes lots of money for Roxanne's grandfather.

c Roxanne and the bear love to go running together after school.

d The film crew comes to the village to film a pop video.

C **What do you think?**

Is Bruno happy living in the cage? Talk about your answer to a partner.

Word detective

A Find three words in the story that end in **–ly**.
Write them here.

_____

_____

Now turn these words into adverbs by adding **–ly**.

bad   terrible   hungry

_____

_____

Remember these rules when adding **–ly**:

If a word ends in 'le' (e.g. gentle), drop the 'e' and add 'y' (gently).

If a word ends in 'y' (e.g. easy), change the ending to 'ily' (easily).

B Find these time words in the story. Write the page number where you found the words.

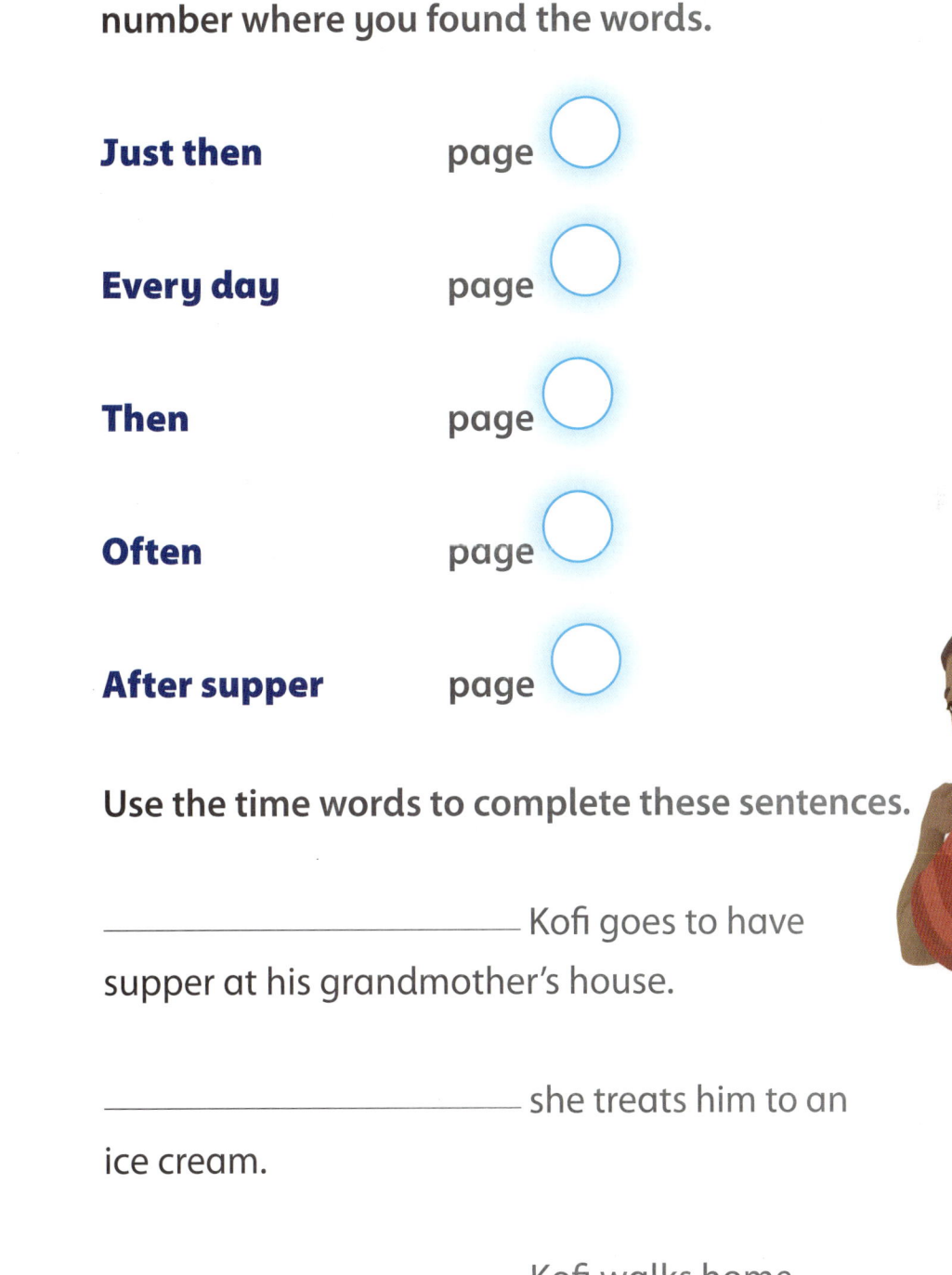

Just then   page ⃝

Every day   page ⃝

Then   page ⃝

Often   page ⃝

After supper   page ⃝

Use the time words to complete these sentences.

_____ Kofi goes to have supper at his grandmother's house.

_____ she treats him to an ice cream.

_____ Kofi walks home.

C Write the words and phrases next to either Roxanne or her grandfather. Add some descriptions of your own.

> **tight-fisted old goat**   **grumbling**
>
> **pure magic**   **interested in money**
>
> **fantastic singer**   **kind to Bruno**

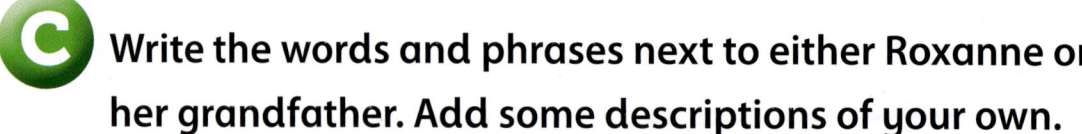

Get writing

Part A Story plan

Think about a story in which a boy or a girl finds a wild animal and keeps it as a pet.

What is your character called?

What type of animal does your character find?

Where does he or she find the animal?

Where does he or she keep the animal?

What does his or her parents or carers say?

Part B Story plan

Use the questions below to help you plan your story.

Beginning

Start your story off: say who your character is and where they find the animal. Is the animal dangerous? How does your character get the animal home?

Middle

What happens next? Describe where the character hides the animal. Write what your character's parents or carers say. Say what the character and animal do together.

End

How will your story end? Perhaps the animal scares away a bully or a robber. Will the character take the animal back to the place where it was found or to a zoo, or will they keep it?

Read your story plan to make sure that you have a good beginning, middle and ending.

Western lowland gorilla

Ivory-billed woodpecker

Let's Talk

If you could save only one of these animals from extinction, which one would it be? Explain why.

Northern right whales

Amazing Leatherback Turtle Facts

Ⓐ Read and respond

Answer these questions.

1 Where do leatherback turtles lay their eggs?

_____

2 How deep can leatherback turtles dive?

_____

3 In which year were there more female turtles laying eggs?

_____

Ⓑ Read and respond

Write one reason why the turtles are dying.

_____

_____

_____

Animals in Danger

 Read and respond

Draw a line to show where each bit of information appears.

Information

'Amur leopard' (words in red)

'The Javan rhino has skin that looks like armour.'

'Hunters kill the rhino for sport.'

Where it is found

Caption

Chart

Subheading

B Read and respond

Use the anthology charts to answer these questions.

1 How many Amur leopards are left in the world? ◯

2 Where does the Javan rhino live? _____

3 Tick the problem that is true for both the Amur leopard and the Javan rhino.

◻ They are killed by hunters.

◻ They don't have enough to eat.

◻ They are killed for medicine.

Word detective

> Reports about living things are
> written in the present tense.

A Write the missing verb in these sentences.
Look back at pages 80–83 to help you.

1 The Amur leopard _____ in the snowy
forests in Russia.

2 They _____ a long way to find food.

3 The Javan rhino _____ the most
threatened.

4 Workers _____ to make this park as good
as it can be.

B Write two special words to do with animals in danger.

Young Explorers

 **Read and respond**

Circle all the non-fiction features you can find in *Young Explorers.*

index

map

subheading

caption

photo

chart

 **Read and respond**

Match the paragraph description to its subheading. The first one has been done for you.

Subheading	Paragraph description
Chilly home	Describes how the big forests are being turned into lots of little forests so the red pandas find it hard to travel between them
Hidden pandas	Tells us how people are trying to help the red panda
Trapped!	Explains where red pandas live
What will the future bring?	Explains why red pandas are hard to find

Word detective

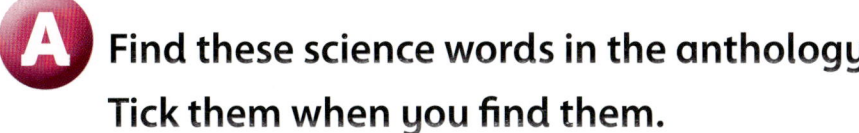

Report texts often have words that are special to the subject.

A **Find these science words in the anthology.**
Tick them when you find them.

bamboo ☐   conservationists ☐

study ☐   replanting ☐   wild ☐

B **Show how each word can be split up into syllables.**
The first one has been done for you.

h i g h / e s t

b a m b o o

r e p l a n t i n g

c o n s e r v a t i o n i s t

Ngorongoro Crater

 **Read and respond**

Answer these questions.

1 Why do people visit the Ngorongoro Crater?

_____

2 Name three animals that live in the Ngorongoro Crater.

_____

3 Why do so many animals like to live in the crater?

_____

4 What might the Maasai farmers need to watch for?

_____

5 Why do the tourists stay in their jeeps and not walk around?

_____

B Read and respond

Find the following places on the map. Tick them when you have found them. Write one thing you would find in each place.

1 Lake Magadi ☐

What can be found here? _____

2 Leral Forest ☐

What can be found here? _____

3 Who or what lives outside the crater?

_____

C What do you think?

What is the purpose of the Ngorongoro Crater text? Share your ideas with a partner.

> Does it tell a story or give information about something?

Word detective

A Fill in the gap in each sentence with the best connective. Use each word once.

> **and   if   because   when**

1 Lions stay inside the crater _____ there is plenty of food.

2 The Maasai people live near the Ngorongoro crater

_____ take their animals into the

crater to give them grass and water.

3 Zebras feel safe _____ they are close to other animals.

4 The tourists are happy _____ they can see lots of animals.

B Adjectives are words used to describe something. Write four adjectives from the report.

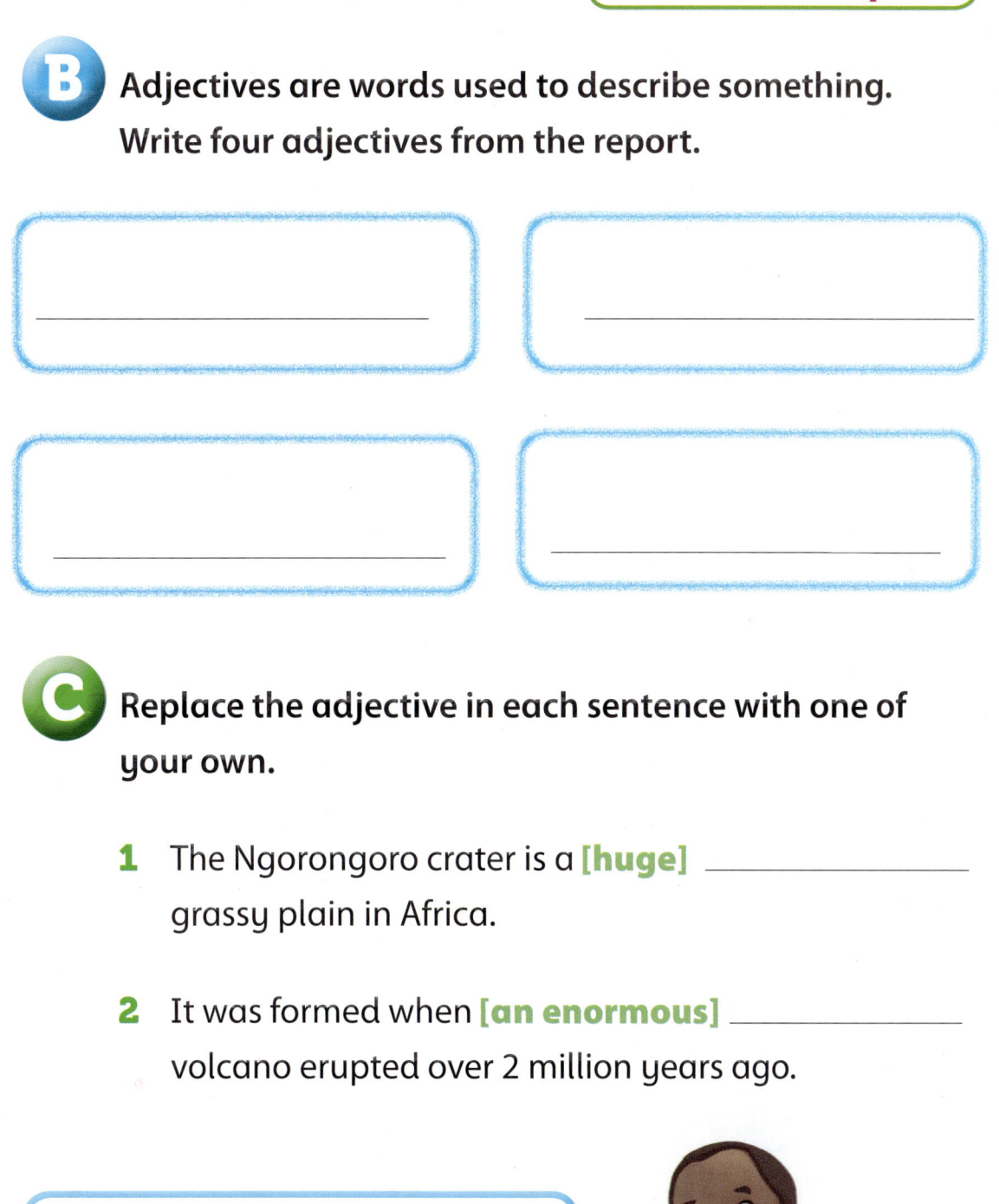

C Replace the adjective in each sentence with one of your own.

1 The Ngorongoro crater is a [huge] _____ grassy plain in Africa.

2 It was formed when [an enormous] _____ volcano erupted over 2 million years ago.

Adjectives are just as important in non-fiction as they are in stories.

Get writing

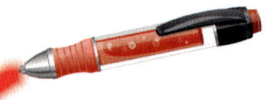

Part A

Write a suitable heading for the text below and add a caption next to the picture.

_____

The Cross River gorilla is the most endangered gorilla. The gorillas are hunted for their meat. There are only about 300 Cross River gorillas left living in the forests in Nigeria and Cameroon in Africa. These forests are being cut down. This means the gorillas get trapped in small sections of forest.

_____

_____

_____

Forest corridors are being created to link the small forests together. National parks protect the Cross River gorilla.

Part B

Put the facts about the Cross River gorilla from **Part A** into the chart.

Look at the charts on pages 81 and 82 of your Anthology to help you.

Cross River gorilla facts

What is the problem?	•
How many are left?	•
Where do they live?	•
How are they being helped?	•
	•

Wordplay poems

Over My Toes

A Read and respond

Answer these questions.

1 Imagine you are the child in the poem. What do you see, feel and hear?

_____

2 What else, apart from the sea, washes over the poet's toes?

_____

3 Read every other line. What is the pattern in the poem?

_____

B Read and respond

Read the poem aloud.

> Use your arms to show the sea washing over your toes and back again in every pair of lines.

Word detective

A Find words that start with **sl**.

sl_____   sl_____   sl_____

Can you think of two more words that begin with **sl**?

_____   _____

B Circle three words that rhyme with '**goes**'.

hose   glows   owls   nose   cows   growls

C Complete these sentences with **see** or **sea**.

1   We went out to _____ in our boat.

2   We could _____ Granny waiting for us.

Name That Dragon

 A Read and respond

Answer these questions.

1 What do you notice about some of the dragon names?

_____

2 Why is 'Sorrow-maker' a good name for a dragon?

_____

_____

3 Are the dragons named in the poem cuddly or scary?

_____

_____

 B Read and respond

Read the poem with your partner.

Clap your hands to show the rhythm as you read.

C What do you think?

What is your favourite dragon name?

Talk to your partner about why you like it.

Word detective

A Find the words that rhyme with these words.

catcher _____   stings _____

taker _____   jaw _____

B Find an adjective from the poem to describe these parts of the dragon.

_____ jaw

_____ fang

_____ wing

_____ tail

Night-lights

A Read and respond

Answer these questions.

1 Which light does the poet think is brighter –
the night-light or the real moonlight?

_____

2 Why isn't the night-light needed?

_____

3 What are the two words that describe the moon's light?

_____   _____

B Read and respond

Tick the box to show if each sentence is true or false.

	True	False
It is a dark night.	☐	☐
The night-light makes a bright light.	☐	☐
The moon is bright and white.	☐	☐

Word detective

A Find the words in the poem that have the long **/igh/** sound.

> Remember – the long **/igh/** sound can be spelt in different ways:

igh in high   **i** in find
y in cry   **i–e** in ice
ie in pie

l_____   n_____

t_____   s_____

m_____   w_____

b_____

Now add the correct letters to make other words with the **/igh/** sound.

fl___   k___nd   cr___ ___d

pr___z___

Get writing

Part A

Use these words to write a list poem about a dragon. Combine one word from each list to create each name.

cave   fire   hero
cloud   treasure

fighter   hoarder
dweller   breather
toucher

Part B

Now with your partner, think of something you would like to write a list poem about. It might be an animal, your favourite food, even your best friend!

> Your words don't have to be made up of two words like the dragon poem. It can be as simple as this:
>   Brown
>   Smooth
>   Cool
>   Sweet
>   Chocolate icecream

_____

_____

_____

_____

_____

What do you think?

Which story, poem or facts did you like best? Draw a picture below of something you enjoyed learning about.

Write two sentences about what you liked best and why.

_____

_____

_____

_____